Zoom In on
Our Renewable Earth

Plants

Andrea Rivera

abdopublishing.com

Published by Abdo Zoom™, PO Box 398166, Minneapolis, Minnesota 55439. Copyright © 2017 by Abdo Consulting Group, Inc. International copyrights reserved in all countries. No part of this book may be reproduced in any form without written permission from the publisher. Abdo Zoom™ is a trademark and logo of Abdo Consulting Group, Inc.

Printed in the United States of America, North Mankato, Minnesota
102016
012017

Cover Photo: Avangard Photography/Shutterstock Images
Interior Photos: Avangard Photography/Shutterstock Images, 1;
Sing Kham/Shutterstock Images, 4–5; Shutterstock Images, 6–7, 7, 8, 10, 11, 12, 16–17, 18;
Maximus Art/Shutterstock Images, 9; Leonard Zhukovsky/Shutterstock Images, 14, 15;
Petr Bonek/Shutterstock Images, 19; Gyuszko Photo/Shutterstock Images, 21

Editor: Emily Temple
Series Designer: Madeline Berger
Art Direction: Dorothy Toth

Publisher's Cataloging-in-Publication Data
Names: Rivera, Andrea, author.
Title: Plants / by Andrea Rivera.
Description: Minneapolis, MN : Abdo Zoom, 2017. | Series: Our renewable Earth |
    Includes bibliographical references and index.
Identifiers: LCCN 2016948925 | ISBN 9781680799392 (lib. bdg.) |
    ISBN 9781624025259 (ebook) | ISBN 9781624025815 (Read-to-me ebook)
Subjects: LCSH: Plant conservation--Juvenile literature. | Conservation of natural
    resources--Juvenile literature. | Renewable energy sources--Juvenile literature.
Classification: DDC 333.95--dc23
LC record available at http://lccn.loc.gov/2016948925

Table of Contents

Science 4

Technology. 8

Engineering 10

Art 14

Math 16

Key Stats. 20

Glossary 22

Booklinks 23

Index 24

Science

Plants are
living things.

Scientists guess that there are 400,000 kinds of plants. But new **species** are still being found.

A plant makes its own food. It gets energy from sunlight.

The energy combines with water and air to make food.

Plants grow in soil. Sometimes **fertilizer** is mixed into soil.

Fertilizer can also be spread while watering. It gives plants more **nutrients**. The nutrients help plants grow.

Greenhouses help plants grow in harsh weather.

They are covered
with glass or plastic.

Light can
pass through.
So can heat.
The greenhouse
stays warm.
Plants can
grow inside.

Art

Florists turn flowers into art.
One company has a flower show.

The flowers are shaped to look like things. They might look like a dress or an animal.

Math

Bees **pollinate** plants. A bee can visit 5,000 flowers in a day.

One bee could visit 50,000 blueberry flowers in its life.

Those plants would make more than 6,000 blueberries.

Key Stats

- Plants cannot get water through their leaves. They get water from their roots. It is important to water the ground where roots grow.

- To know if a plant needs water, check the soil. If it forms into a ball in your hand, do not add water. If the soil crumbles, it is time to water.

- Plants grow at different rates. Some kinds of bamboo can grow almost 3 feet (0.9 m) in a day.

Glossary

energy - power that living things use to move or grow.

fertilizer - chemicals that are added to soil to help plants grow.

nutrient - an essential food that plants or animals need to grow.

pollinate - to transfer pollen from one plant to another. This allows the second plant to produce seeds.

species - one of the groups that animals and plants are divided into.

Booklinks

For more information
on plants, please visit
booklinks.abdopublishing.com

 In on STEAM!

Learn even more with the Abdo Zoom
STEAM database. Check out
abdozoom.com for more information.

Index

air, 7

bees, 16, 18

energy, 6, 7

fertilizer, 8, 9

flowers, 14, 15, 16, 18

food, 6, 7

greenhouses, 10, 13

nutrients, 9

scientists, 5

soil, 8

species, 5

sunlight, 6, 13

water, 7, 9